D1273498

GLAMOUR BY DESIGN

DESIGN DRAWINGS FROM THE HOUSE OF

COUTURIER

16, AVENUE MATIGNON
PARIS

1925-1948

by

EMILY BANIS STOEHRER

JEAN S. AND FREDERIC A. SHARF COLLECTION
MUSEUM OF FINE ARTS BOSTON

ACKNOWLEDGEMENTS

This book would not have been possible without the generous support of Frederic A. Sharf, a trustee at the Museum of Fine Arts, Boston (MFA). Fred purchased the Lucien Lelong archive for the museum and spearheaded this research project and book. He has an avid interest in history and the preservation of archival materials, particularly those related to design.

I am incredibly grateful to Pam Parmal, the David and Roberta Logie Curator of Textile and Fashion Arts, and Yvonne Markowitz, the Rita J. Kaplan and Susan B. Kaplan Curator of Jewelry, at the MFA. Both women offered me guidance, encouragement, and support throughout this project.

I owe an enormous debt of gratitude to Jacqueline Demornex. Her meticulously researched book, *Lucien Lelong*, was essential in placing these drawings in the context of Lelong's career and in understanding his business practices. Similarly, research done by Sarah Scaturro and Sonya Mooney for *Modern Master: Lucien Lelong, Couturier 1918-1948*, a 2006 exhibition at the Museum of the Fashion Institute of Technology (MFIT), was essential in pointing me towards key sources on Lelong. Scholarship on twentieth century fashion, such as Caroline Evan's *The Mechanical Smile*, Lou Taylor's essay "Paris Couture: 1940-1944" in *Chic Thrills: A Fashion Reader*, and Dominique Veillon's *Fashion Under the Occupation*, helped to contextualize the group of Lelong drawings.

The FIDM Museum is home to an extensive collection of Lelong perfume, makeup, and ephemera. The museum's blog entries on Lelong, written by Meghan Grossman Hansen, were also invaluable to my understanding the development of Lelong's beauty business. I am also grateful to the FIDM Museum's curator, Kevin Jones, who explained to me the role similar drawings played for Betsy Bloomingdale.

I would also like to thank the following people for assisting with research, providing information and photos, and encouragement along the way: The Chicago History Museum, Paul Cyr, Michelle Tolini Finamore, Pierce MacGuire, Marjorie Phillips, Steve Sdatny, Meridith Spencer, Mark Stoehrer, and Lauren Whitley.

—Emily Banis Stoehrer

"Meli Mélo"
Winter 1925

Copyright © Emily Banis Stoehrer 2013

All rights reserved. No part of this work may be reproduced or utilized in any form or by any means, electronic, mechanical, including photocopying, recording or by any information or retrieval system, without the prior written permission of the publishers.

This publication was printed and bound by Velocity Print Solutions, Middlebury, CT

ISBN-10: 0-9839573-9-8
ISBN-13: 978-0-9839573-9-3

Library of Congress Control Number:
A catalog record for this book is available from the Library of Congress.

FIRST EDITION

Printed in the United States of America

Table of Contents

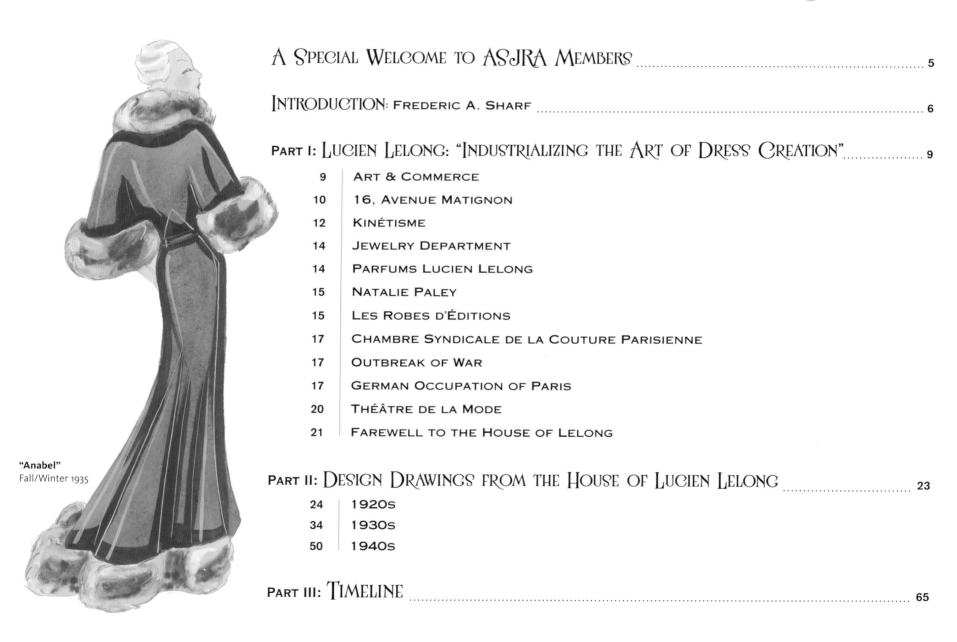

"Anabel"
Fall/Winter 1935

LUCIEN LELONG
16, AVENUE MATIGNON — PARIS

Mlle Suzanne

NOM DU MODÈLE :

LUCIEN LELONG
AVENUE MATIGNON — PARIS

NOM DU MODÈLE :

Lady

N° 3

Modèle Déposé
Reproduction Interdite

2999

KINDLY RETURN AS SOON AS POSSIBLE THE
SKETCHES WITH HAVE NOT BEEN CHOSEN

PRIÈRE DE VOULOIR BIEN RETOURNER LE PLUS
TOT POSSIBLE LES DESSINS NON CHOISIS

Modèle Déposé
Reproduction Interdite

2998

KINDLY RETURN AS SOON AS POSSIBLE THE
SKETCHES WITH HAVE NOT BEEN CHOSEN

PRIÈRE DE VOULOIR BIEN RETOURNER LE PLUS
TOT POSSIBLE LES DESSINS NON CHOISIS

A SPECIAL WELCOME TO ASJRA MEMBERS

The Association for the Study of Jewelry & Related Arts (ASJRA) thanks Fred Sharf and Emily Banis Stoehrer for making this beautiful book available to ASJRA members.

As an association dedicated to the study of jewelry history, we strongly advocate that jewelry not be studied in a vacuum. ASJRA takes a broad approach to the subject, seeking to understand and place jewelry within a variety of contexts, including from the ancient past to present day, the decorative arts, and perhaps most importantly, fashion.

We use jewelry as a window into the study of cultures and specific time periods as it reveals a great deal about politics, cultural changes, world events, stylistic trends, materials, technologies, and usage.

For jewelry historians, fashion and adornment are inextricably bound together within a given time period. They are part of a whole and the study one provides clues to the other.

Jewelry is often designed to match necklines, hang properly on various fabrics, and work with popular hair-styles and/or with hats. Anyone who approaches jewelry history without placing it within the context of fashion is missing a major portion of the "snapshot" that jewelry offers of a time period.

Fred Sharf has made it his mission to salvage the archives of both jewelers and couturiers alike, making them available to the general public so they can be both appreciated and used as a tool to understand the past.

With this publication, Emily Banis Stoehrer has made the story of Lucien Lelong come to life as she did for jeweler Louis Féron in the previous volume she and Fred created and graciously made available to ASJRA members.

We are grateful to both of them.

Yvonne Markowitz
Elyse Zorn Karlin
ASJRA Co-Directors

above: **Necklace and Finger Ring**
Spring 1935

opposite: **"Lady"**
Winter 1934

INTRODUCTION

FREDERIC A. SHARF

"Cairo-ca'
Winter 1934

In mid-April 2012 a Parisian couturier, Dominique Sirop, contacted Pam Parmal Logie Curator of Textile and Fashion Arts, Museum of Fine Arts, Paris.

Dominique wanted to sell the museum a vast fashion archive which included original design drawings and back issues of fashion magazines. Pam reviewed the offering and concluded that there were too many items of no interest to the museum.

She asked me to follow up with Dominique about the fashion drawings, some of which would fit nicely into the MFA collection. Since she had no funding available she hoped I might be able to make a deal with Dominique for some lots.

I decided to send my London representative, Leslie Verrinder, to Paris in early June to review the drawings. He identified two groups which stood out in his mind—Lucien Lelong, and Madeleine et Madeleine. Both groups had great visual appeal, and important scholarly value. I purchased these two groups in June 2012.

After they arrived, Emily Stoehrer looked them over and asked if I could set them aside until the summer of 2013. She was working on the Louis Feroñ jewelry drawing archive in the summer of 2012. Her book on this archive was published in January 2013.

Emily has been an important part of my life since the spring of 2010. She was working as an intern in the MFA fashion department. The museum admired her sense of style, and her research skills. I sent her to Gstaad, Switzerland in August 2010 to review the archive of Andrew Grima. Andrew was one of the stars of post-WWII British jewelry design. His archive included design drawings, documents, letters, and photographs.

Emily returned with a detailed and very enthusiastic report. Andrew Grima's wife and daughter decided against providing us with access. They did not want a book at that time.

Lucien Lelong has been a terrific project for Emily. She scanned 525 drawings. Most had been organized by year under Dominique's supervision in Paris. With three exceptions they were all drawn on Lelong letterheads in a combination of goache, ink and pencil. An unknown artist working in Lelong's studio drew detailed, fully accessorized figures wearing the new style for that season.

The drawings were meant to be used by a vendeuse (saleswoman) in the salon to show clients. Many drawings depicted a named ensemble, accompanied by a fabric swatch, a handwritten description, and often even the price.

The vast majority of these drawings had been done for a vendeuse named Suzanne. The vendeuse was a key link between the couturier and his client. Clients often became devoted to their vendeuse. She helped with the selection process, and was present for the many fittings required by the couturier. The drawings were an important sales tool. They introduced the collection to a prospective client, indicating colors available, as well as materials.

It is very unusual for such a large group of design drawings to survive. Once the season ended, most of these drawings would have been discarded. Some customer of Suzanne saved her drawings, and they are now housed at MFA, Boston. In addition, they will be thoroughly researched by Emily, and published.

These drawings celebrate the career of Lucien Lelong. Few American museums have any Lelong drawings so the fact that this large group is available digitally will be an incredible resource for scholars.

Frederic A. Sharf
September, 2013

"Bouboule"
Spring 1935

"Tessa"
Spring/Summer 1935

LUCIEN LELONG:
"INDUSTRIALIZING THE ART OF DRESS CREATION"

"Vedette"
Winter 1925

opposite: **Henry Sell and Lucien Lelong**
November 7, 1925
National Photo Company Collection
© Library of Congress

THE FRENCH HAUTE COUTURIER LUCIEN LELONG WAS BORN IN PARIS ON OCTOBER 11, 1889. His parents, Arthur and Eleanor owned A.E. Lelong, a successful dressmaking shop on Rue Vignon in Paris. His uncle was a textile merchant. You could say that Lucien had fashion in his blood!

In 1898, the Lelongs moved their shop to a more fashionable location at Place de la Madeleine, and expanded overseas, opening a shop on Hanover Square in London. Their British clients included Queen Victoria. Years later, in 1911, as their business continued to grow, the Lelongs joined the *Chambre Syndicale de la Couture Parisienne*, the watchdog of the couture industry whose role is to maintain the standards of the haute couture and to dictate who can use the coveted title, couturier or couturière. The specific rules that govern couture houses have changed with time but some things remain—original made-to-measure designs are hand finished in *ateliers* in the city of Paris using traditions handed down by generations of artisans. This was how Lucien Lelong was introduced to his craft. His knowledge of aesthetics was paired with a specialized education at Paris's finest business school, École des Hautes Études Commerciales. He graduated in 1913.

In 1914, Lucien Lelong designed his first collection, but when war was declared on August 4th, he was forced to cancel his show. Instead, he was drafted into the French army. Lucien served in the Intelligence branch of the army where he tracked the movements of the German army until he was wounded by shrapnel in May 1917. Injured, he returned to Paris. His wounds were serious enough to require an extensive recovery period. When the war finally ended in November 1918, Lucien, eager to revisit his design career, returned to the family business.

A.E. Lelong had remained open during the war years, but by 1919 the firm was nearly bankrupt. Lucien encouraged his parents to retire and in 1919 he took charge of the business. To rebuild the firm and recover financial losses, he took in a partner named Fried. Fried presumably supplied the funding needed to keep the business going. For a brief time the house was renamed Lelong et Fried, but by 1921 Lucien was in complete control. That year his new collection was favorably received by the press and the House of Lelong was properly launched.

ART & COMMERCE

The fashion press was quick to appreciate the newness of the Lelong designs. His work was described as modern, streamlined, fluid, youthful, and with a new word—kinetic. The dresses that Lelong launched in the 1920s were no doubt inspired by his early life and experiences. He grew up handling fine fabric and, examining meticulously handsewn dresses. Lelong likely became accustomed to dealing with an elite clientele who would later become his patrons. Outside the doors of his parents thriving establishment, Paris was abuzz with art and culture. Lucien Lelong participated in the cultural world of Paris before the war when Poiret created dresses meant to be worn without a corset, and the *Ballet Russes* produced vibrant dances in revolutionary costume. After the war, he mingled with a new group of young people who went to nightclubs and to dance halls.

The totality of his experiences was embodied in the designs, which the press admired. He was conscious of the way in which a woman's body moved in her clothing and wanted to design dresses that were easy to wear. Lelong

Untitled
Winter 1925

was certainly in touch with the zeitgeist of the post-war era. He assembled a team of designers to work with him and oversaw the entire design process with a meticulous eye for detail. He understood the key to building a successful brand was about more than good design; it needed to be rooted in sound business practices. Under Lelong's careful leadership the small business he inherited from his parents grew quickly. By 1924 he employed 1200 people.

Above all, Lucien Lelong was a keen businessman. Instead of studying at a liberal arts university, he elected to go to business school. With its highly focused curriculum, École des Hautes Études Commerciales gave Lelong the tools necessary to build a successful empire. Despite lacking the romance of a university campus, the school taught Lelong the importance of understanding business practices and leadership skills. This, coupled with his frequent visits to the United States during the twenties and thirties, where he studied the garment industry, allowed him to bring a fresh perspective to the time-honored traditions of the haute couture.

16, AVENUE MATIGNON

The 1920s were a successful decade for the young designer and 1924 proved to be a pivotal year. At the age of 35, Lelong relocated and expanded his thriving business, moving from his parent's salon at 18 Place de la Madeleine to a sprawling *hôtel particulier* (a grand-style townhouse) at 16 Avenue Matignon. The move positioned Lelong closer to the fashionable rue Montaigne where Madeleine Vionnet and many other couturiers were centered. Nestled between the Champs-Élysées and Rue du Faubourg Saint-Honoré, Lelong's new space was said to be the "largest dressmaking plant in Paris."[1]

In describing the new space, Lelong appropriated an industrial vocabulary foreign to the hand-craftsmanship of the haute couture. In the renovated space, Lelong installed the latest technological innovations such as forced ventilation, elevators, and telephones. The designer also built an eight-story "factory" in space that was formerly a "court-like garden."At this sprawling new facility, he worked toward "industrializing the art of dressmaking."[2] Lelong believed that within a year he would have 3,000 employees, making his firm nearly twice the size of his peers! His success in Paris led to further expansion and he added showrooms in the resort towns of Biarritz and Cannes.

The House of Lelong's new space was certainly impressive, but equally inventive was the way Lelong showed his collections. In the grand salon, fashion shows included state-of-the-art lighting that flaunted dresses in an array of different light levels from natural daylight to twilight. Spotlights further highlighted dazzling details like jeweled skirts and embroidered dresses. Nothing was left to chance. Chairs were numbered and ushers shuttled guests to their assigned seats. From a high stool Lelong oversaw each fashion show's production. He would coolly approve each design before sounding a buzzer that allowed the model, known in the couture house as a *mannequin*, to walk the illuminated runway. The House of Lelong became known as a place where a variety of tastes were considered. Lelong would often show the same model with subtle variations—sleeveless and sleeved, for example.

Amid Lelong's expansion and the success of his collections, he quietly registered a new branch of the company, Parfums Lucien Lelong. Beginning in the 1920s couturiers started adding perfume to their list of offerings. The decision proved a moneymaker for the business, as it was inexpensive to produce and offered steady revenue. The introduction of perfume made the Lelong name accessible to a wider audience of women who desired the brand's chic, but couldn't afford to buy haute couture fashions. As Lelong developed his plans for the diversification and marketing of his brand, 1925 brought new opportunities for the firm.

[1] Robert Forrest Wilson, "The House of Lucien Lelong," 15 October 1925 *Vogue*, 33-36.
[2] Ibid 35. In 1925 *The New York Times* claimed this "skyscraper was actually nine-stories high.

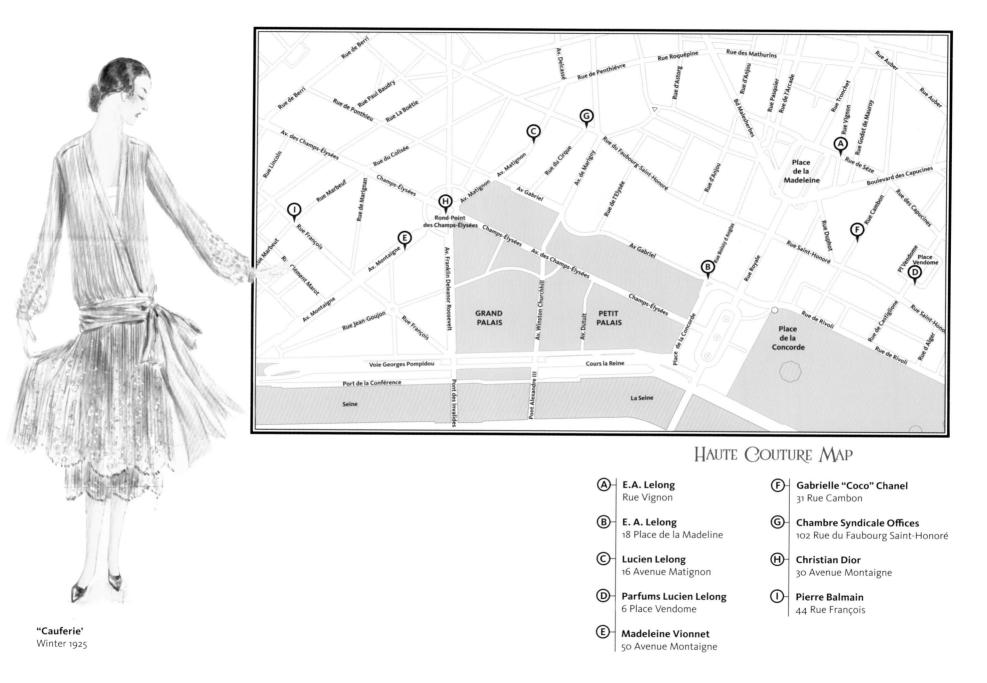

"Cauferie'
Winter 1925

HAUTE COUTURE MAP

(A) **E.A. Lelong**
Rue Vignon

(B) **E. A. Lelong**
18 Place de la Madeline

(C) **Lucien Lelong**
16 Avenue Matignon

(D) **Parfums Lucien Lelong**
6 Place Vendome

(E) **Madeleine Vionnet**
50 Avenue Montaigne

(F) **Gabrielle "Coco" Chanel**
31 Rue Cambon

(G) **Chambre Syndicale Offices**
102 Rue du Faubourg Saint-Honoré

(H) **Christian Dior**
30 Avenue Montaigne

(I) **Pierre Balmain**
44 Rue François

Fashion Show Program
Lucien Lelong
Spring 1932

KINÉTISME

After being rescheduled multiple times, the *Exposition Internationale des Arts Décoratifs et Industriels Modernes*, opened in April of 1925. Lelong and other couturiers showcased their latest collections in the Pavilion de l'Elégance. Here, Lelong not only displayed his newest designs but also introduced clients to a new design theory he called *kinétisme*. In touch with the spirit of the times, Lelong sought to bring the decade's dynamism to life by creating clothing that emphasized freedom and motion. These dresses accentuated the decade's slim two-dimensional silhouette, short hairstyle, and newly painted faces by incorporating layers of transparent and opaque textiles. To achieve fluidity, Lelong used a variety of dressmaker details such as cutting on the bias; incorporating added fullness with box pleats, panels, or godets; and embellishments like beads, fringe, and jeweled embroidery.

The ideology was detailed and marketed in advertisements that ran in publications such as *Vogue*. In July he outlined "My Plans For Fall":

> In our studio we design gowns in motion. The picture we seek to make is the picture the gown presents when passing. All cut, decoration, and arrangement of color are directed to that end. Incidentally, it gives that extreme ease of movement—that wearability—to a gown that the modern sportswoman demands. [3]

Such manifestos brought media attention and Lelong's embrace of modernism was consistently reported in the American press.

Inspired by dancing dresses, Lelong hoped kineticism to be embraced for day and eveningwear by a modern woman on-the-go. Compared to styles of the recent past, these dresses were incredibly risqué, often showing the wearer's legs (and sometimes her knees!). They could also be low cut with merely a translucent panel of chiffon covering the décolletage and often exposing the arms and back. While other couturiers were designing similar dresses, Lelong's theoretical approach set him apart. More than mere dresses, Lelong's *kinétisme* can be viewed as a form of conceptual art—*la femme* as art.

---

[3] Lucien Lelong, "My Plans for Fall," *Vogue,* 15 June 1925, 7.

"Ma Joie"
Winter 1925

"Doucie Amie"
Winter 1925

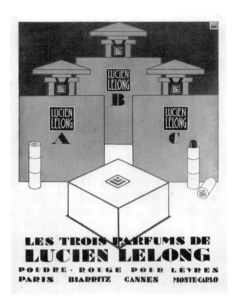

Perfume Advertisements
1920s and 1930s

JEWELRY DEPARTMENT

Equally important in outfitting the Lelong woman was her jewelry. Like hats and shoes, jewelry completed a woman's ensemble, but historically women who could afford to purchase haute couture dresses flaunted real gemstones and precious metals. In the 1920s, inspired by Gabrielle "Coco" Chanel, women began mixing real and costume jewels. Lelong was among the first couturiers to embrace this trend and in 1925 added a costume jewelry department where he sold adornments to compliment his seasonal styles.

Since the early twenties, Lelong's designs had been noted for their jeweled and beaded accents. A flower placed at the low-slung hip of his dresses had become a signature element. The addition of a formal department was a logical progression. In addition to selling items like necklaces, earrings, and bracelets, he also incorporated such decorations directly into his designs. Dress with plunging necklines were reportedly filled in with spangles, while others included embroidered elements like a sautoir with a "swinging rhinestone tassel," sleeves with wide bracelet-like embroidery, and yokes embroidered with rhinestone necklaces.[4]

PARFUMS LUCIEN LELONG

As Lelong's business continued to grow he was finally ready to introduce his first perfume. Despite registering the company Parfums Lucien Lelong in 1924, he did not launch his first scent until 1926. The addition proved so successful that Lelong opened a separate shop at Place Vendôme that was dedicated to perfume and make-up. In 1928, Lelong even opened a boutique in Chicago.

Perfume was also meant to complete a woman's ensemble. The incorporation of fragrance was good for business as it increased sales; provided greater visibility for the brand; and allowed for retail space, filled with signature scents, to entice customers from the sidewalk. Women were encouraged to own a variety of scents to suit their changing look and mood.

After two years of careful planning, Lelong launched not one but three perfumes in 1926. Mysteriously named A, B, and C—collectively they were known as "Tout Lelong" (or in English "All Along Lelong")—each corresponded to a particular time of day. Lelong went on to design over twenty scents. Among his most popular was Indescret, launched in 1935. Its bottle reflected the sculptured drapery of his couture salon and mimicked the look of a draped and pleated skirt or a rising curtain with the front showing a slight lifting of the drapery. His perfume Elle Elle provided a double entendre playing with Lelong's initials, L.L.

Niches were designed in his salons to display the glass perfume bottles. The packaging often proved as interesting as his scents. To inspire sales and generate renewed interest in the brand, Lelong introduced special seasonal designs and limited editions. At Christmas, fur covered tubes of lipstick and bottles adorned with ringing bells replaced the customary designs. The beauty business was so profitable that his Place Vendôme showroom continued to thrive even after Lelong closed his couture house.

---

[4] "Paris Presents Gemmed Gown," *The New York Times*, 19 June 1927, X8.

"Auteuil"
Spring/Summer 1935

right: **Lucien Lelong and Natalie (Paley) Lelong**
Chicago Daily News, 1927
© Chicago History Museum

NATALIE PALEY

As Lelong worked to expand his brand's image during the twenties, his marriage to the Russian princess Natalie Paley proved to be successful both personally and professionally. Paley, a member of the Romanov family, was the daughter of Grand Duke Paul Alexandrovich of Russia and a first cousin of Czar Nicholas II. After the Russian Revolution, Paley moved to France where she, like many Russian émigrés who were forced to find work, saw haute couture as an appealing option. She reportedly worked at Lelong as a model and "saleswoman in his perfumery department" before marrying Lelong in 1927.[5] The Lelongs honeymooned in the United States where they likely mixed business with pleasure. The couple's time in Chicago was probably spent lining up distributers and planning the launch of the city's Lucien Lelong boutique.

Mrs. Lucien Lelong came to embody the House of Lelong's ideal client. Her constant appearance in society and fashion magazines gave her celebrity status. Paley and her circle of friends, which included the ultra-fashionable Princess Jean-Louis de Faucigny-Lucinge (better known as Baba), generated a renewed interest in the House of Lelong. Baba was said to have fittings at Lelong each Thursday. Since her every move was reported on in the fashion press, her connection to Lelong fueled the company's success during the early thirties.

---

[5] "Lucien Lelong Weds Russian Princess," *The New York Times*, 11 August 1927, 24.

LES ROBES D'ÉDITIONS

Lelong had been studying the American ready-to-wear industry since his first visit to the United States in 1925. In 1934 Lelong launched a prêt-à-porter (ready-to-wear) collection. Titled *Les Robes d'Éditions*, the garments—sold as limited editions—were shown in a new wing on the first floor of Lelong's couture house. Lelong was said to have collaborated with clothing manufacturers to produce the ready-to-wear collection and to keep costs down. Evening dresses reportedly sold for upwards of 300 francs, a fair bit cheaper than the 2500 francs a tailored day dress from his couture operation cost that same year. These designs were available in five sizes and custom options were available; clients could pay 50 francs for alterations or 100 francs for two fittings. But his ready-to-wear model failed to find success and Lelong continued to be puzzled by the ability of American department stores to sell ready-made clothing to thousands of consumers.

"Incroyable"
Fall/Winter 1934

right: **"Mille Raies"**
Spring 1936

Even with the failure of *Les Robes d'Éditions*, the 1930s were a decade of great achievement for the House of Lelong. Clients eager to emulate the most fashionable women of the day were keen to obtain a Lucien Lelong ensemble. Despite press that sometimes described his collections as tired, many saw the thirties as the pinnacle of his career. Lelong's tailored dress and jacket combinations for daytime, sportswear ensembles, and romantic evening dresses continued to be in style when endorsed by fashion leaders like Baba and Mrs. Lucien Lelong. Other clients during the thirties included Wallis Simpson, who later became the Duchess of Windsor; Mrs. Harrison Williams, who in 1933 was voted the best-dressed woman in the world; film stars like Marlene Dietrich; and even *Vogue* staffers Bettina Ballard and Mrs. Stanley Mortimer ("Babe" Paley after her second marriage). Unfortunately, Lelong's marriage to Natalie Paley ended in divorce in 1937, but their partnership had a lasting impact on his success.

CHAMBRE SYNDICALE DE LA COUTURE PARISIENNE

By 1937, Lelong had spent a lifetime in the fashion business. After celebrating sixteen years as an arbiter of fashionable tastes, he was held in the highest esteem by his peers. When a vacancy arose at the *Chambre Syndicale de la Couture Parisienne*, his colleagues recognized his business acumen and elected him chairman.

Lelong's role as a leader in the organization began unofficially in the 1920s with his series of expeditions to the United Sates. During his time abroad he not only studied the growing American fashion industry, but served as an ambassador of French fashion. His travels throughout the country were tracked by the press, as were his professional appearances with organizations such as the Garment Retailers of America. His suave demeanor and commitment to the French haute couture made him a natural successor when the Chairman Pierre Garber resigned in 1937.

Once Chairman, Lelong faced challenges almost immediately. New labor laws in France meant the haute couture needed to revise many of their practices. In addition, new American tax laws made the cost of importing couture garments prohibitive for many clients. Lelong faced an uphill battle even before the declaration of war in September of 1939.

OUTBREAK OF WAR

Uncertain how the war would impact the country, many couture houses closed temporarily, but re-opened a month later. The months from autumn of 1939 to the spring of 1940 were known as "the phoney war." Little had changed in Paris and fashion carried on uninterrupted. At first, Americans were reluctant to travel to Paris to see the mid-season collections in November. However, with peaceful conditions in Paris in the early months of 1940, and the persistent reports by newspapers such as *The New York Times*, which encouraged France to continue exporting

luxury items, the *Chambre Syndicale* was able to convince some important American buyers to come for the spring collections in 1940.

As leader of the *Chambre Syndicale* Lelong was a key decision maker for the haute couture and he was optimistic. But the German military advances in May and the certainty that Paris would be conquered by mid-June shattered Lelong's confidence. France surrendered. A peace treaty with Germany was signed on June 22, 1940. Lelong left Paris before the treaty was signed and moved to Biarritz where he shared a studio with fellow couturiers Elsa Schiaparelli and Edward Molyneux. The trio had even arranged housing for their staff with the idea of completely relocating there for the remainder of the war.

GERMAN OCCUPATION OF PARIS

In June, an armistice between France and Germany was signed and France was a country divided. The Nazi occupied zone was centered in Paris and included Northern France and the coastline. A free zone was established at Vichy under the government of Philippe Pétain. In August the Germans demanded that all businesses in the occupied zone reopen, or they would be seized. Lelong had kept his Paris business running under the capable management of Émilie Dupas. Lelong returned to Paris in mid-July. On Sunday July 28 the Germans broke into the offices of the *Chambre Syndicale* and stole the archives, as well as current files and customer lists. Lelong thus had two immediate worries: how to keep his own business going and how to recover the *Chambre Syndicale's* documents.

German troops settled into their new role in France and set out to re-organize the French fashion and textile industries. Lelong was named Managing Director of the couture section of the newly created Textile Committee. The Germans proposed to move the couturiers to Berlin or Vienna. Lelong was outraged and told Germans that the haute couture would never leave Paris. In November of 1940, he traveled to Berlin to make his case directly to

"Kobette"
Spring 1936

"Hermione"
Winter 1940

"Un Coeur Ardent"
Possibly Winter 1942

"Bonne adventure"
Winter 1942

Nazi leadership. Lelong succeeded in gaining their cooperation—the haute couture would remain in Paris and the stolen files would be returned. Lelong's goals during the remainder of the war were unwavering. He sought to keep the couture industry's skilled workers employed and to maintain the haute couture's reputation abroad.

Lelong negotiated with the Nazis to create a system of supplying the couture houses with the raw materials needed to carry on their business. Eighty-five couture houses were recognized. Each was allowed 60% of the amount of fabric that had been used during the same month in 1938. In November of 1941, the number of authorized houses was reduced to 71 and in September 1943 it was further cut to 54. With an artificial exchange rate invented by the Germans, shopping in France was very advantageous. There was a steady influx of wealthy Germans, senior military officers, film stars, and returning clients who came to Paris to shop. While Lelong and others undoubtedly benefited from this favorable exchange rate, they later claimed that very few of their wartime clients were German.

Lelong worked to preserve the entire couture establishment while at the same time maintaining his own business. During the Occupation the House of Lelong groomed two emergent design talents. Pierre Balmain had joined the House of Lelong in 1938, left after the outbreak of war, and returned in 1941. That same year another designer, Christian Dior, joined him. During the 1940s, the two designers would produce what some considered the couture house's best collections.

Throughout the Occupation, Lelong walked a fine line, maintaining the goals of the haute couture, while also appeasing German leadership in Paris. He was asked by the German Institute to show a collection there. The institute had been created in 1940 to enhance the German presence in Paris. It offered language classes, and cultural attractions—all were naturally in German. Lelong was also among the few elite Parisian couture houses that had the

dubious pleasure of welcoming the Nazi leader Hermann Göring and his wife Edda to their salons during one of the couple's many trips to the city. In March 1942, Lelong organized a very successful fashion show in Lyon. More than 350 buyers came from neutral counties—Spain, Portugal, Turkey, Switzerland, and North Africa—to see the latest French designs. That same year, Lelong sent Balmain to exhibit on behalf of the House of Lelong at the International Exhibition in Barcelona.

While Lelong's business seemingly flourished the rest of the world suffered from shortages of materials and daily life restrictions. By the beginning of 1942, Paris too faced shortages and tensions rose in the Occupied area. Leather was no longer available and women were forced to wear shoes made of alternative materials with raised heels and articulated soles. As a way of thumbing their nose at such conditions, French woman began wearing outrageous hats. Such fashion statements were the female way of telling Germans that France would not be defeated! Anxiety increased as French Jews were suddenly forced to wear a large yellow six-pointed star on their lapels and French citizens began being sent to Auschwitz. A delicate balance existed in the couture houses of Paris. Fear was ever-present, especially after a member of the Rothschild family was "sent to Ravensbruck concentration camp" after refusing "to sit next to the wife of a Nazi official" at a fashion show.[6] Slowly, an entire portion of the French population was disappearing.

Paris was liberated in 1944. Despite negative press coverage and "whispers of collaboration," Lelong managed to meet his wartime goals and the haute couture, although much reduced and forever changed, survived World War II.[7]

---

[6] Lou Taylor, "Paris Couture 1940-1944," *Chic Thrills: A Fashion Reader*, (London: Pandora, 1992), 130.
[7] Ibid 135.

Winter 1943

THÉÂTRE DE LA MODE

As chairman of the *Chambre Syndicale*, Lelong played a key role in reconstructing the industry's image. After four years of Occupation and rumors of collusion with the Nazis, the French people were determined to rise from the ashes, restore the reputation of France, and secure the future of Parisian fashion. With the economy in shambles, the French fashion industry needed to plan something drastic to assure its future. As the war continued to be fought in much of Europe, the fashion designers of Paris set to work on a project they felt would restore their standing as the world's fashion center and serve as a "poetic symbol of hope and renewal."[8] In a period where materials continued to be scarce, Paris couturiers produced an unimaginable feat.

Lelong and other fashion designers donated their time and worked together to raise money for France. A competitive spirit filled the air as more than two hundred fashion dolls emerged from the haute couture's *ateliers*. The results not only spoke to the accomplishments and creative spirit of dress designers, but also of hairstylists, jewelers, milliners, and all the craftspeople of the small *ateliers*—the embroiderers, feather dressers and flower-makers whose work supported the couture. The dolls were installed on thirteen stages and exhibited in Paris' Pavillon de Marsan at the Louvre from March until May of 1945. The installation then went on to tour Europe and the United States, attracting nearly 100,000 visitors.

[8] Stanley Garfinkel, "Théâtre de la Mode: Birth and Rebirth," *Théâtre de la Mode, Fashion Dolls: The Survival of Haute Couture*, (Portland, OR: Maryhill Museum of Art, 2002), 41.

"Lucree"
Spring/Summer 1947

FAREWELL TO THE HOUSE OF LELONG

Lelong's long and illustrious career came to a close in the post-war period. After the war, Lelong was tried and acquitted of Nazi collaboration. Increasingly, he was viewed by his peers in Paris and New York as the savior of the haute couture—a legacy that survives today. After working tirelessly for nearly three decades, Lelong's health began to fail. He retired from his position as Chairman of the *Chambre Syndicale* in 1945. His tireless efforts on behalf of French fashion led the organization to appoint him honorary chairman for life.

Fashion had come full circle. Lelong began his career during a time when fashion was avant-garde and forward thinking. Not surprisingly, he chose to retire as it became increasingly nostalgic. After the war, Lelong's protégées Pierre Balmain and Christian Dior left to open their own couture houses. Both men preferred a corseted look and nineteenth century inspired silhouette that was at odds with Lelong's modern aesthetic. In the spring of 1948, Lelong presented his last haute couture collection and closed his business on Avenue Matignon in the summer of that year. His successful perfume business remained in operation at Place Vendôme. After his retirement, Lelong moved to Anglet, near Biarritz. It was there that he died of a heart attack in 1958. In his obituary in *The New York Times* provided a fitting epitaph calling him the "unofficial dictator of the world's female fashions." [9]

Today Lucien Lelong is best remembered for his leadership during the Occupation. However, his talents and contributions to the fashion industry are far more extensive. Lelong was an astute arbiter of fashionable tastes. Working to modernize the French fashion industry he juxtaposed art and commerce and succeeded in building a world-renowned fashion business. The careful construction of his brand as well as his brilliant business practices led Lelong to become one of the most famous and respected couturiers of his day.

■

---

[9] "Lucien Leong, 68, Fashion Designer," *The New York Times*, 12 May 1958, 29.

"Valse Rose"
Spring/Summer 1946

"Vision"
Spring/Summer 1948

Design Drawings from the House of

"Maya"
Spring/Summer 1935

The Lucien Lelong drawings that make up the Jean S. and Frederic A. Sharf Collection span from 1925 to Lelong's final collection in 1948. For more than twenty years their format remained consistent. The drawings, which measure ten inches tall and six and three-quarter inches wide, have Lelong's name and address in the upper left corner—all date from after his move to 16, Avenue Matignon. The group of drawings from 1925 includes the additional description, "Rond-point des Champs-Élysées," noting Lelong's location near the Champs-Élysées' traffic circle, but by 1932 the added line was removed. In the upper right corner under a printed headline that reads "nom du modèle" is the handwritten name of each ensemble. The garment's name is sometimes inspired by current events, music, theatre, art, or literature. At the lower left corner is the phrase "modèle déposés," and below "reproduction interdite." These notations act like a patent for the design. They identify that it has been registered with the *Chambre Syndicale de la Couture* and that it is not to be reproduced. Across the

page, in the opposite corner, marked in both English and French is: "Kindly return as soon as possible the sketches which have not been chosen." The client presumably kept the drawings for styles she selected.

The drawings are executed with extraordinary attention to detail. The talented draftsmen who depicted Lelong's fashions included appropriate accessories, jewelry, hairstyles, and makeup to complete each look. In the 1920s corresponding garments—like coats and dresses—are found on one page, but by the 1930s a separate page is used to show each look. In the forties the reverse of an ensemble is sometimes depicted on the back of a drawing. Many of the drawings also bear additional handwritten notations: detailed descriptions related to style and materials, a fabric swatch, the name of the client's *vendeuse*, a price, and after WWII sometimes even information on taxes. Viewed as a whole this large collection of drawings, with its combination of text and imagery, provide viewers a careful picture of the House of Lelong's aesthetic.

1920s

The twenties introduced Lucien Lelong as a creative *tour de force*. His designs were favored by many of the most fashionable women in the world and were continuously noted for their clean lines and movement. Lelong was seen as a designer whose streamlined style was deceptively simple and always modern. The drawings from the twenties are isolated to 1925, but even this small sampling allows viewers get a sense why journalists were so impressed. Coverage in the fashion press details minute shifts in the way Lelong's skirts and dresses moved; in February of 1925, *The New York Times* reported that Lelong "created the outward movement of the skirt." In April, *Vogue* called attention to his "double-purpose" dresses that easily moved from afternoon to evening and his "pocket handkerchief" dresses that folded effortlessly into a weekend bag. His startling color combinations—such as black and pink—were also highlighted.

The drawing style works to convey the layering of fabrics, ease and mobility, and the resulting *kinétisme*. The illustrations depict women with the newly fashionable short hairstyles and makeup. While skirts reached their shortest proportions around 1927, with hemlines falling to the knee, in 1925 the slightly-below-the-knee length was shorter than any other previous period in fashion's history. Lelong's short dresses are accessorized with earrings or long strands of pearls wrapped around the neck or wrists. Often the dresses themselves are also jeweled, and some include a low-slung diamond belt buckle or beaded embroidery. The tradition for furs, a signature of Lelong's parents, continued into the 1920s with fur-trimmed coats and dresses with fur hemlines.

■

LUCIEN LELONG
16, RUE MATIGNON — PARIS
(ROND-POINT DES CHAMPS-ÉLYSÉES)

NOM DU MODÈLE :

Ratounet

Dressy ensemble in black Satin or black cloth and red crepe chine with gold & silver embroidery. Satin coat trimmed with gold opposum

dress 2000

) Coat. 3200

(without fur. 2000.

The coat with grey astrakan.

3800

MODÈLE DÉPOSÉ
REPRODUCTION INTERDITE

KINDLEY RETURN AS SOON AS POSSIBLE THE SKETCHES WHICH HAVE NOT BEEN CHOSEN

PRIÈRE DE VOULOIR BIEN RETOURNER LE PLUS TOT POSSIBLE LES DESSINS NON CHOISIS

"Ratounet"
Winter 1925

LUCIEN LELONG
16, RUE MATIGNON — PARIS
(ROND-POINT DES CHAMPS-ÉLYSÉES)

NOM DU MODÈLE :

Matinal

Ensemble in cloth, very nice lines. The dress has pleats on the side. Coat in same material trimmed with grey astrakan

dress 1400

) Coat. 2400.

(without fur 1800

MODÈLE DÉPOSÉ
REPRODUCTION INTERDITE

KINDLEY RETURN AS SOON AS POSSIBLE THE SKETCHES WHICH HAVE NOT BEEN CHOSEN

PRIÈRE DE VOULOIR BIEN RETOURNER LE PLUS TOT POSSIBLE LES DESSINS NON CHOISIS

"Matinal"
Winter 1925

"Un Ieu"
Winter 1925

"Vlan"
Winter 1925

LUCIEN LELONG

16, RUE MATIGNON — PARIS

(ROND-POINT DES CHAMPS-ÉLYSÉES)

NOM DU MODÈLE:

nice little
dress in iberia
collar & cuffs
embroidered
in gold
on a mauve
crepe

2200.

KINDLEY RETURN AS SOON AS POSSIBLE THE
SKETCHES WHICH HAVE NOT BEEN CHOSEN

MODÈLE DÉPOSÉ
REPRODUCTION INTERDITE

PRIÈRE DE VOULOIR BIEN RETOURNER LE PLUS
TOT POSSIBLE LES DESSINS NON CHOISIS

"Petit Daille"
Winter 1925

LUCIEN LELONG

16, RUE MATIGNON — PARIS

(ROND-POINT DES CHAMPS-ÉLYSÉES)

NOM DU MODÈLE:

3600

KINDLEY RETURN AS SOON AS POSSIBLE THE
SKETCHES WHICH HAVE NOT BEEN CHOSEN

MODÈLE DÉPOSÉ
REPRODUCTION INTERDITE

PRIÈRE DE VOULOIR BIEN RETOURNER LE PLUS
TOT POSSIBLE LES DESSINS NON CHOISIS

"Jádore çà"
Winter 1925

"Caline"
Winter 1925

"Caline"
Winter 1925

"Frelon"
Winter 1925

Winter 1925

"Arlequin"
Winter 1925

Winter 1925

"Idylle"
Possibly Winter 1925

"Javotte"
Winter 1925

"Sourire"
Winter 1925

"Vogue"
Winter 1925

"Indécise"
Winter 1925

"Flore"
Winter 1925

1930s

Many view the 1930s as the pinnacle of Lelong's success and his biographer calls it his "finest decade." While many Americans, in the midst of economic depression, reduced or eliminated their luxury purchases, an elite clientele—who become known as café society—continued to splurge on made-to-measure ensembles by the artists of the haute couture. During the thirties, Lelong embraced a youthful aesthetic, doing away with unnecessary ornamentation and pursuing a slim tailored silhouette for daytime—suits, dresses and coats with asymmetrical details—and romantic eveningwear. His high-profile marriage to Natalie Paley resulted in his work being constantly represented in the media.

Lelong continued to advocate for modernism, telling *The New York Times*, "The gestures that went with a Watteau fan are not appropriate for the steering wheel...it [fashion] is a creation of the present for the future, and has no need to be colored by the past." However, his thirties dresses include a few eighteenth century references. Examples include "Blue Boy," a tailored day dress named after the iconic Thomas Gainsborough painting, and "Pompadour" with two bows at the neckline reminiscent of Madame de Pompadour's preferred *échelle*-style stomacher that had a vertical row of bows. Such designs always work to highlight the feminine curves of the wearer and never distort the body.

The collection of Lelong drawings includes examples from 1932, 1934, 1935, 1936, and 1939. These thirties designs include longer hemlines and strong—sometimes voluminous—shoulders juxtaposed by slim hips. Feminine details like large bows and lace were incorporated into day and evening designs, sportswear was highlighted, and unexpected color combinations and dazzling details continued to generate interest.

■

"Frileuse"
Winter 1934

"Blue Boy"
Winter 1934

"Péronnelle"
Winter 1932

"Treluche"
Winter 1932

"Sylvia"
Winter 1932

"Irillés"
Winter 1932

"Nocturne"
Winter 1932

"Bergerade"
Winter 1934

LUCIEN LELONG
16, AVENUE MATIGNON — PARIS

NOM DU MODÈLE :

Fragonard

Comme le modèle —

5196

MODÈLE DÉPOSÉ
REPRODUCTION INTERDITE

KINDLY RETURN AS SOON AS POSSIBLE THE
SKETCHES WITH HAVE NOT BEEN CHOSEN

PRIÈRE DE VOULOIR BIEN RETOURNER LE PLUS
TOT POSSIBLE LES DESSINS NON CHOISIS

"Fragonard"
Winter 1934

LUCIEN LELONG
16, AVENUE MATIGNON — PARIS

En faille rose
N° 22

col 1   col 2

NOM DU MODÈLE :

Little Woman

Little Woman
Robe du soir en faille
rose, bas de la robe
garni de biais en même
tissu que la robe.
Fleurs de velours corail

2959

MODÈLE DÉPOSÉ
REPRODUCTION INTERDITE

KINDLY RETURN AS SOON AS POSSIBLE THE
SKETCHES WITH HAVE NOT BEEN CHOSEN

PRIÈRE DE VOULOIR BIEN RETOURNER LE PLUS
TOT POSSIBLE LES DESSINS NON CHOISIS

"Little Woman"
Winter 1934

"Cordoba"
Winter 1934

"Aiglonne"
Winter 1934

"Fréjus"
Spring/Summer 1935

"Challenge"
Spring/Summer 1935

"Maya"
Spring/Summer 1935

"Mac. Midie"
Spring/Summer 1935

left — right **"Jouvencelle"**
Spring/Summer 1935

"Makalla"
Fall/Winter 1935

"Louqseor"
Fall/Winter 1935

"Anita"
Fall/Winter 1935

"Un Caprice"
Fall/Winter 1935

"Virginie"
Fall/Winter 1935

"Pompadour"
1936

"Cadette"
Spring 1936

"Antonia"
Spring 1936

left — right **"Zig Zag"**
Fall/Winter 1936

"Indiscret"
Fall/Winter 1936

"Volage"
Spring 1936

1940s

The forties are a complex decade and Lelong's work bears witness to shifting styles seen during the early years of the 1940s, the war years, and the post-war era. The drawings include Lelong's work from 1940, 1942, 1943, 1946, 1947, and his final collection in 1948. Beginning in 1940, the number of models shown by couturiers was greatly reduced. Despite disruptions to both travel and communication, some buyers were able to travel to Paris in November 1939 for the mid-season collections and some also arrived for the spring shows in early 1940. As tensions ran high, evening dresses evoked nostalgia and daytime attire was cut close to the body. Lelong's day dresses remained tailored with a strong and sometimes puffy shoulder for both day and evening. Ensembles included feminine details like bows, flounces, rosettes, and sweetheart necklines. Surprisingly, some historic sewing techniques, such as cartridge pleating (a nineteenth-century technique re-introduced in Dior's New Look collection in 1947), also appeared in Lelong's designs from the forties.

Despite the restrictions placed on couturiers by the Germans, Lelong's designs during the Occupation, created by Pierre Balmain and Christian Dior, continued to have his tailored and streamlined style and continued to include eveningwear with long hemlines and wide skirts. The period's large hats were a defiant statement against Nazi restrictions. However, the drawing style shows a more severe woman than those illustrated before the war. Lelong's collections became more austere and the drawings are deprived of color by the middle years of the decade.

In 1946, dresses once again became luxurious and sculptural with draped necklines and sashes tied into a large bow or knotted at the waist. Hips were accentuated by wide full or slim fitted skirts that emphasized small waists and many of the designs were accessorized with a beaded choker and earrings. By Lelong's final collection, the Second Empire styles he resisted for so long had taken hold and his final collections show an aesthetic at odds with the modernity he advocated during the twenties and thirties. Such historically influenced styles would come to define Christian Dior's New Look and continue to evolve in the 1950s.

■

left — right **"Cocarde"**
Fall/Winter 1939-1940

"Muriel"
Fall/Winter 1939-1940

"Aero"
Fall/Winter 1939-1940

"Katty"
Fall/Winter 1939-1940

"Pour moi"
Fall/Winter 1939-1940

LUCIEN LELONG
16, AVENUE MATIGNON — PARIS

Suzanne

NOM DU MODÈLE
Ami fidèle

tailleur 9500
blouse 2300

*Tailleur lainage
gris, garni velours
gris.*

7985

MODÈLE DÉPOSÉ
REPRODUCTION INTERDITE

KINDLY RETURN AS SOON AS POSSIBLE THE
SKETCHES WITH HAVE NOT BEEN CHOSEN
PRIÈRE DE VOULOIR BIEN RETOURNER LE PLUS
TOT POSSIBLE LES DESSINS NON CHOISIS

LUCIEN LELONG
16, AVENUE MATIGNON - PARIS

Suzanne.

NOM DU MODÈLE
Heureux retour

6.900

*Cette robe crêpe mat
orchidée (à rentrer)
peut se faire en
différents tons
foncés ou clairs
à l'échantillon.*

41

MODÈLE DÉPOSÉ
REPRODUCTION INTERDITE

KINDLY RETURN AS SOON AS POSSIBLE THE
SKETCHES WITH HAVE NOT BEEN CHOSEN
PRIÈRE DE VOULOIR BIEN RETOURNER LE PLUS
TOT POSSIBLE LEE DESSINS NON CHOISIS

"Ami Fidèle"
Winter 1942

"Heureux refour"
Winter 1942

"Dans la Maison"
Winter 1942

"Lettre d'amour'
Winter 1942

"Pélléas"
September 1943

September 1943

"Watteau"
Winter 1946

"Azur"
Spring/Summer 1946

"Delrileuse"
Spring/Summer 1946

"Shopping"
Winter 1946

"Caprice"
Winter 1946

"Fête galante"
Winter 1946

"Envol"
Fall/Winter 1947

"Contrat"
Fall/Winter 1947

"Regis"
Spring/Summer 1947

"Elma"
Spring/Summer 1947

left — right **"Amphytrion"**
Spring/Summer 1948

"Corsaire"
Spring/Summer 1948

"Barbara"
Spring/Summer 1948

"Bergamasque"
Spring/Summer 1948

"Tour de hae"
Spring/Summer 1948

"Incroyable"
Winter 1934

1889 October 11	Lucien Lelong is born in Paris to Valentine Éléonore Marie Lambelet and Arthur Camille Joseph Lelong owners of A.E. Lelong on Rue Vignon in Paris
1898	E.A. Lelong moved to 18, Place de la Madeleine
1905 January 21	Dior is born
1908	Colette's *Les Vrilles de la Vigne* is published; The story's heroine, Valentine, is described as wearing designs by Lelong
1909	Lelong serves in the 4th Hussar Regiment of the French military
May	*Ballet Russes* first performs in Paris
1911	E. A. Lelong joins the *Chambre Syndicale de la Couture Parisienne*
1911-1913	Lucien Lelong attends business school at École des Haures Études Commerciales located in Paris
1914 May 18	Pierre Balmain is born
Aug 2	France mobilizes troops for World War I
Aug 4	Lucien Lelong was scheduled to show his first collection but declaration of war forces cancelation; Lelong joins the 2nd Cuirassier Regiment
1915 January 22	Appointed Reserve Second Lieutenant
1917 May 24	Wounded in "the frontline trench" with shrapnel damaging his right side and left hand; awarded French Military Cross; hospitalized for 9 months

"Ambassade"
Winter 1934

1919	Lelong returns to work at his parent's couture house
1920	A.E. Lelong is renamed Lelong et Fried; Lelong and his wife Anne-Marie Audoy welcome a daughter, Nicole
1921	Lelong et Fried is renamed House of Lucien Lelong
1924	Relocates to 16, Rue Matignon; registers Parfums Lucien Lelong
1925	Lelong travels to United States to study the ready-to-wear industry
April – Oct	*Exposition Internationale des Arts Décoratifs et Industriels Modernes* (International Exposition of Modern Industrial and Decorative Arts); Lelong introduces kinétisme in the Pavilion Elegance and is one of the few couturiers whose name is mentioned in the official government report
1926	Launches A, B, and C perfumes
1927	
July	Lelong and Audoy divorce
August 9	Lelong marries Natalie Paley at Saint-Alexndre Nevski a Russian Orthodox cathedral in Paris; The couple honeymoon in New York
	Launches J (for Jasmine) and N (for Natalie) perfumes with bottles designed by René Lalique
1928	Lelong perfumes opens in Chicago
1929	
October 29	Wall Street stock market crash
1930	Introduces an inspection department at his couture house to assure perfection in every garment that was sold
1934	
October	*Vogue* announces that the launch of *Les Robes d'Éditions*
c. 1936	Lelong showrooms are redesigned in all white
1935	Indiscret is launched

"Zani"
Spring 1936

August	Sails aboard the *Normandie* for its maiden voyage
1936	Jean Schlumberger works briefly as the Director of Perfume at Lelong's Place Vendôme salon; Couture workers go on strike demanding a 40 hour work week, two weeks of paid vacation per year, and higher wages
June 8	Settlement is reached with couture workers ending strike
1937 June	M. Gerber resigns as chairman of the *Chambre Syndicale de la Couture Parisienne* and is replaced by Lelong
	Spends six weeks in the United States
	Lelong provides readers of *Votre Beauté* with a dress pattern in an attempt to reach a wider audience
	Lelong and Paley divorce; Paley moves to America and marries the producer John Chapman Wilson and works for the fashion designer Mainbocher
1938	Rents a studio in Montparnasse and begins sculpting
September	Munich Agreement is signed
	Balmain beings working for House of Lelong
1939 Sept 1	Germany invades Poland
September 3	France and England declare war with Germany after German troops refuse to pull forces out of Poland; Couture houses are forced to close temporarily
October	Couture houses reopen with limited staff
	Balmain is mobilized by the French army
1940 January 8	Rationing begins in Britain
March	Lelong convinced some American buyers to travel to see Paris collections; those in attendance

"Peusés"
Spring 1936

	arrive in Paris by train from Italy
May 10-June 21	Battle of France
May 26	Evacuation of Allied troops from Dunkirk, Belgium
May 28	Belgium surrenders
June 10	Italy declares war on France and Britain
June 13	Paris declared an "open city" and government flees to Bordeaux
June 14	Germans enter city of Paris; Lelong temporarily relocates to Biarritz; Charles de Gaulle flees to London and founds the resistance movement
June 14-25	Remaining British troops leave France
June 16	Marshal Pétain becomes French Prime Minister at Bordeaux
June 22	Armistice between France and Germany is signed
July 20	Five Nazi officers arrive at *Chambre Syndicale* headquarters at 102, Rue du Faubourg Saint-Honoré to gather information on the state of the French haute couture
July 28	The Nazis outline a plan to move the couture to either Berlin or Vienna
July 29	Lelong assures couturiers that the haute couture will continue as normal despite Occupation and will work to employ as many people as possible
November	Lelong and Daniel Gorin (*Chamber Syndicale* secretary) travel to Berlin to argue against relocating the couture
1941 October 6	Dior begins work at Lelong
December 1	Balmain returns to work at Lelong
1942	

"Volage"
Spring 1936

March	Lelong organized a fashion show in Lyon, France and invited 350 industry professionals from Spain, Portugal, Switzerland, and North Africa
	Balmain represents the House of Lelong at the International Exhibition held in Barcelona
1944 June 6	D-Day invasion on Normandy Beaches via air and sea; more than 10,000 Allied soldiers are killed but 100,000 successfully enter France
August 19-25	Battle for Paris
August 25	Liberation of Paris by allied forces
	Autumn collections are called "excessive" by foreign press who are outraged at the spectacle of fashion on the streets of Paris; Lelong replied explaining that this was an expression of defiance and that the ruffles and makeup hid gaunt cheeks and threadbare dresses
November 15	Lelong issues an apology to American readers of *Vogue* explaining that he only just heard of wartime restrictions; outlines French restrictions as: 1. Forty models per collection 2. Small percentage allowed in wool blends 3. Fabric limitations: 3 ¼ meters of fabric per dress, 3 ¾ per suit, 4 ¼ per coat
	Balmain leaves the House of Lelong to open his own couture house on Rue François and took Lelong seamstress Juliette and model Praline with him
1945	Lelong tried and acquitted of Nazi collaboration
	Readers of *Vogue* and *Harper's Bazaar* are encouraged to buy French goods as a way of supporting the war effort
March to May	*Théâtre de la Mode* on display in Paris before traveling to European and American cities
May 8	Victory in Europe Day
May	Lelong travels to United States to reestablish connection between American and French industries
November 5 **1946**	Lelong resigns as chairman of the *Chambre Syndicale* and is appointed honorary chairman for life Introduces perfume Orgueil

"Peusés"
Spring 1936

December 1	Dior leaves Lelong and is briefly replaced by Givenchy
December 16	Dior founds couture house at 30, Avenue Montaigne and hires Lelong's studio director Raymonde Zunacker
1947	Lelong's daughter Nicole drops out of medical school and begins working for her father
1948 Feb 4	Lelong's final collection
July	Closed couture house amid failing health; perfume salon at 6, Place Vendôme remains open
1949	Debuts Cachet Bleu perfume
1954	Lelong marries for the third and final time to Sandra Dancovici and moves from Paris to Anglet (near Biarritz)
1957 October 23	Dior dies unexpectedly of a heart attack
1958 May 11	Lelong suffers a heart attack and dies; his obituary in *The New York Times* called him the "unofficial dictator of the world's female fashions" during the 1930s

THE MFA/SHARF
AUTOMOTIVE AND FASHION HISTORY BOOK COLLECTION

Richard H. Arbib, 1917-1995: Visionary American Designer
Format: Hardcover
Pages: 64
ISBN: 1-882266-16-1

American Automobile Art, 1945-1970:
Drawings from the Great Age of American Car Design
Format: Softcover
Pages: 80
ISBN: 978-1-882266-19-7

Carl Renner:
1950s GM Dream Car Creator
Format: Hardcover
Pages: 64
ISBN: 978-0-9818865-9-6

Larry Salk: California Dreaming
and the Evolution of American Fashion Art: 1945-1965
Frederic A. Sharf with Susan Ward
Format: Softcover
Pages: 64
ISBN: 1-882266-18-8

Style and the City: New York City Fashion Art
Two Decades of Advertising Drawings: 1955-1975
Frederic A. Sharf with Morton Kaish
and Alexandra B. Huff
Format: Softcover
Pages: 72
ISBN: 978-0-9818865-6-5

Beauty as Duty
Textiles on the Homefront of WWII Britain
Alexandra B. Huff with Frederic A. Sharf
Format: Hardcover
Pages: 80
ISBN: 978-0-9839573-0-0

Britain Can Make It
Postwar Progress Through Determination,
Innovation & Exploration
Frederic A. Sharf with Sheldon Steele & Anne Vallely
Format: Hardcover
Pages: 64
ISBN: 978-0-9839573-3-1

Future Retro:
Drawings from the Great Age of American Automobiles
Museum of Fine Arts Publications, Boston, MA 2005
Format: Hardcover
Pages: 80
ISBN: 0-87846-690-8

Harry Bentley Bradley:
American Automotive Design Innovator
Format: Hardcover
Pages: 64
ISBN: 978-09818865-0-3

Fisher Body Craftsman's Guild, 1930-1968
John L. Jacobus and Ronald J. Will with Frederic A. Sharf
Format: Softcover
Pages: 64
ISBN: 978-0-981-8865-2-7

Theodore Pietsch II (1912-1993) and the Development of
Automobile Design in the Golden Age
Theodore W. Pietsch III with Foreword by Frederic A. Sharf
Format: Hardcover
Pages: 80
ISBN: 978-0-9818865-5-8

Studebaker's Last Dance: The Avanti
Andrew Beckman with Foreword by Frederic A. Sharf
Format: Hardcover
Pages: 64
ISBN: 978-0-9839573-2-4

American Fashion Art 1960-1990
Three Decades of Advertising Drawings
Frederic A. Sharf with Susan Ward
Format: Softcover
Pages: 64
ISBN: 978-0-9818865-3-4

Exploring Fashion
The Art of Kenneth Paul Block 1960-1990
Susan Mulcahy with Frederic A. Sharf
Format: Hardcover/Softcover
Pages: 64
ISBN: Hardcover: 978-0-9818865-7-2
      Softcover: 978-0-9818865-8-9

Fabric/Figure/Fantasy
Five decades of American fashion drawing (1940s-1980s)
Alexandra B. Huff and Frederic A. Sharf
with Phil French and Morton Kaish
Format: Hardcover
Pages: 104
ISBN: Hardcover: 978-0-9839573-1-7

Louis Féron Master Jeweler 1901-1998
Paris, Costa Rica, New York
Emily Banis Stoehrer and Frederic A. Sharf
Format: Hardcover
Pages: 80
ISBN: 978-0-9839573-4-8

The Fashionable Nurse
A Study of Stylish Professional Dressing, 1910-1970
Frederic A. Sharf with
Catherine Pate & Jill Carey
Format: Hardcover
Pages: 64
ISBN: 978-0-9839573-5-5

John Bates: British Fashion Designer
The Sensational Years, 1963-1968
Frederic A. Sharf with Michelle Finamore
Format: Hardcover/Softcover
Pages: 64
ISBN: Hardcover: 978-0-9839573-6-2
      Softcover: 978-0-9839573-7-9

The Lifestyle of New York Cafe Society, 1935-1950
as Drawn by Jaro Fabry
Frederic A. Sharf
Format: Hardcover
Pages: 72
ISBN: 978-0-9839573-8-6